This book is a gift to:

_____

Message:

_____

_____

_____

_____

_____

From:

_____

Blessings of Grace

© 2013 Christian Art Gifts, RSA
        Christian Art Gifts Inc., IL, USA

Art © Bethany Berndt-Shackelford, licensed by Suzanne Cruise

Designed by Christian Art Gifts

Scripture quotations are taken from the *Holy Bible*, New International Version® NIV®. Copyright © 1973, 1978, 1984, 2011 by International Bible Society. Used by permission of Zondervan Publishing House. All rights reserved.

Scripture quotations are taken from the *Holy Bible*, New Living Translation®, second edition. Copyright © 1996, 2004, 2007 by Tyndale House Publishers, Inc., Carol Stream, Illinois 60188. All rights reserved.

Scripture quotations are taken from the New King James Version. Copyright © 1979, 1980, 1982 by Thomas Nelson, Inc. Used by permission.All rights reserved.

Scripture quotations are taken from the *Holy Bible*, English Standard Version. Copyright © 2001 by Crossway Bibles, a division of Good News Publishers. Used by permission. All rights reserved.

Scripture quotations are taken from the New Revised Standard Version Bible. Copyright © 1989 the Division of Christian Education of the National Council of the Churches of Christ in the United States of America. Used by permission. All rights reserved.

Printed in China

ISBN 978-1-4321-0735-2

14 15 16 17 18 19 20 21 22 23 – 11 10 9 8 7 6 5 4 3 2

Blessings of Grace

MESSAGES

to Encourage & Inspire

christian
art gifts®

MAY

GRACE & PEACE

BE YOURS IN

ABUNDANCE

{2 Pet. 1:2}

GRACE is the free,
undeserved GOODNESS
and favor of God to mankind.

MATTHEW HENRY

TO EACH ONE
OF US

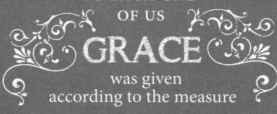

GRACE

was given
according to the measure

of Christ's gift.

[Eph. 4:7]

Nothing whatever pertaining to

GODLINESS and real **HOLINESS**

can be accomplished without grace.

THE LORD

IS MY

STRENGTH & SHIELD.

I **TRUST** HIM WITH ALL **MY HEART.**

HE **HELPS** ME **&** MY **HEART**

is filled

with joy.

{Ps. 28:7}

Grace keeps us from worrying

because worry **DEALS** with the past,

while grace deals with the

PRESENT and **FUTURE.**

Joyce Meyer

THE

LORD

be with your

Spirit

Grace be with

YOU.

(2 Tim. 4:22)

Your **WORST** days are
never so bad that you are beyond the
reach of God's **GRACE**.
And your **BEST** days are never
so good that you are beyond the
NEED of God's grace.

JERRY BRIDGES

GOD IS

gracious &
compassionate,

SLOW TO ANGER

AND ABOUNDING IN

love

{JOEL 2:13}

GRACE:

God's **RICHES** at

Christ's Expense.

ANONYMOUS

―――――――♦―――――――

A state of **MIND** that sees

God in **EVERYTHING** is evidence

of growth in grace and a

THANKFUL heart.

CHARLES FINNEY

My

grace

IS SUFFICIENT
FOR **YOU.**

FOR MY

power

IS MADE PERFECT IN

WEAKNESS.

[2 COR. 12:9]

Let your **speech**
always be
Gracious,

seasoned with **salt,**
so that you may know how
YOU ought to answer

EVERYONE

{COL. 4:6}

The greater **PERFECTION**

a soul **ASPIRES** after,

the more dependent it is

upon **DIVINE GRACE.**

BROTHER LAWRENCE

Grace comes into THE SOUL,
as the morning SUN into the world;
first a dawning; then a LIGHT;
and at last the sun in his full
and EXCELLENT brightness.

THOMAS ADAMS

IN HIM

we have

redemption

through **His** blood,

the **forgiveness** of sins,
in accordance with the riches
of **GOD'S** grace.

[Eph. 1:7]

HE GIVES US

GRACE & GLORY

The Lord will withhold
no *good thing* from those
who do what is

right

{Ps. 84:11}

Natural **STRENGTH** is

what we receive from the

HAND of God as Creator.

Spiritual strength is what we

receive from God in **GRACE**.

WATCHMAN NEE

The **BRIDGE** of
grace will bear your weight.
Thousands of big sinners have gone
ACROSS that bridge, yes, tens of
thousands have gone **OVER** it.
I will go with them trusting to the
same support. It will **BEAR** me
over as it has for them.

CHARLES H. SPURGEON

The Lord

fulfills the desires of those
who **fear** Him;

& He hears their cry and
SAVES THEM.

(Ps. 145:19)

FROM HIS

{ ABUNDANCE }

we have all **received** one
GRACIOUS BLESSING
after another.

{JOHN 1:16}

Amid the **DARKNESS**
of sin, the **LIGHT** of God's
grace shines brightness.

ANONYMOUS

THE LORD

is compassionate and
merciful,

---

slow to get angry
and filled with
UNFAILING LOVE.

{Ps. 103:8}

As grace is **FIRST** from God,

so it is continually from Him,

as much as **LIGHT** is all day long

from the sun, as well as at **FIRST**

DAWN or at **SUN-RISING**.

JONATHAN EDWARDS

LET US THEN

with confidence draw near
to the throne of *grace*,

that we may receive

mercy

and find grace to help in
time of *need.*

{Heb. 4:16}

The **LAW** works fear and wrath;

grace works **HOPE** and

MERCY.

MARTIN LUTHER

For it is by **grace**

you have been saved, through

Faith

and this is not from
yourselves, it is the

GIFT OF GOD.

{Eph. 2:8}

If you **LIVE** close to God and

His **INFINITE** grace,

you don't have to tell;

it shows on **YOUR FACE.**

Anonymous

PREPARING YOUR MINDS

for action

and being sober-minded, set your **HOPE**
fully on the grace that will be brought

to you at the revelation of

JESUS CHRIST

{1 Pet. 1:13}

God doesn't just **GIVE** us grace,

He gives us Jesus,

THE LORD of grace.

JONI EARECKSON TADA

I TRUST IN YOUR
unfailing love.

I will rejoice because *You*

have *rescued* me.

I will *sing* to
the *Lord* because He is

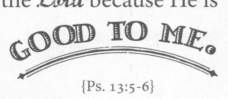

GOOD TO ME.

{Ps. 13:5-6}

I ENTRUST YOU TO GOD

& the message of His *Grace* that is able to build you up

and give you an *inheritance*

with all those He has set apart

FOR HIMSELF

{Acts 20:32}

Where the **WILL** of God **LEADS** you,

the **GRACE** of God will keep you.

ANONYMOUS

GOD IS ABLE

to make all *grace* abound to you,
so that having all *sufficiency*

 IN ALL THINGS
AT ALL TIMES

you may abound

in every good work.

{2 Cor. 9:8}

Free **GRACE** can go

into the gutter,

and bring up a **JEWEL**!

CHARLES H. SPURGEON

KNOWLEDGE is but

folly unless it is

GUIDED by grace.

GEORGE HERBERT

May you experience

THE LOVE
OF CHRIST

though it is too great to
understand fully.

Then you will be made complete

with all the fullness of

LIFE & POWER

that comes from God.

{EPH. 3:19}

MAY
our Lord Jesus Christ
Himself and God our Father,
who loved us and by **His**

Grace

gave us eternal encouragement
AND GOOD HOPE,
encourage your **hearts** and
strengthen **you** in every good
deed & word.

{2 Thess. 2:16-17}

By grace I understand the **FAVOR** of God, and also the **GIFTS** and working of His Spirit in us; as love, **KINDNESS**, patience, obedience, mercifulness, despising of worldly things, **PEACE**, concord, and such like.

WILLIAM TYNDALE

LET US RUN WITH

ENDURANCE

the race that is set before us,
looking to Jesus,

*the founder
and perfecter*

of our faith.

{HEB. 2:1-2}

44

I am not what I OUGHT to be.

I am not what I WANT to be.

I am not what I HOPE to be. But still, I am

not what I used to be. And by the grace of God,

I AM WHAT I AM.

JOHN NEWTON

Grace is **LOVE** that cares

and **STOOPS** and **RESCUES.**

John Stott